Promise Land

VOICES FROM A FUTURE DETROIT

41 Lyrics

Lee Dennis

Promise Land
Voices from a Future Detroit

Beginning

silent streets
dawn light intensifies
above cold ground
fog lingers
hand raised to hush
carried through obscuring drifts
voices from the path ahead

How one among us came to know

A restaurant in Exeter:
across a bright white brass-trimmed room,
they bent and pushed and rose to leave and
fussed with ordinary coats.
But one stood still,

a fine and cleanly hollowed face surrounded by
a modern fall of burnished medieval hair that lightly touched
broad softly sueded shoulders. Above the hands at rest atop
his chair, a multitude of bracelets of steel and silver links –
a quality of stillness, even down to polished boots at
one with polished floor.

Eyes too at rest on one of of them, he waited while she paid his bill.
Who was she then? What quality, what character had captivated him,
what great design, what gift deserved attention such as this,
acceptance, and suspended strength? Or was this not his grant to
her, but rather hers to him?

Somehow stronger than his strength, she marked him so,
a wanted m'an, and from the peopled turbulence,
distilled his very stillness.

What great grandmother said

it's a little hard to understand how a
place with so many churches can be so
godawfully godforsaken

you understand that they
have done the right things
they consulted

with experts and the experts made
recommendations

transportation said the
experts you need
transportation

so they built a little lightweight
toylike train to
nowhere

offices
for those who wear blue collars
and don't know how to read

and small boutiques
for those who drive to
K-Mart

jobs they said you must
attract employers who make
buggy whips

and need a highly
educated work force that
you don't know how to teach

crime they said control the
crooks who want the stuff that's hustled on TV

and drugs and sex, it doesn't help
the image, don't you see, to sell
the only things you've got

well, damn,
let's take this
town and

cut it into
villages
where everybody knows
everybody's only child

and the place you work
you walk to and the
jobs are things like
growing our own food
which takes our brawn
as much as brains
to start and

while we're at it let's declare
girls' rules and girlfriend
village incidentally

let's do all this so that it's
red that is
good for the people
and green that is good
for the planet and
black that is good
for tomorrow if

you unplug yourselves and look
around you sisters what you see
are

a few white diamonds

rare old copper coins

and much much rich
black gold

      with wealth like this
      we can build a
      world we can

Strange attractor

Football fields of blackjack tables
        slot machines, flashing lights, cruising
                cameras perched on walls, action,
                        numbing action.

Sweatshirts, running shoes, plastic cups of
        drinks, of coins, handbags gaping,
                fingers dipping, hands shaking. Overhead,
                        the sign says Change.

Some of the taking leaves the oasis, crosses
        acres of parking lots, stays briefly in town,
                passing through groceries, liquor stores,
                        and lottery shops,

headed for suburban malls. Most comes back
        on its two days off, back to the slots and the
                bingo halls. Suckers aren't born here, we
                        make them ourselves.

Not only quarters, unholy smoke, they leave us their
        sadnesses, misplaced hopes, dreams of diamonds
                and tropic daze, pieces of silver and
                        pieces of soul.

Again tomorrow, the odds be with us, we'll
        flash the lights and ring the
                bells and sell their losses
                        back to them,

keeping the change,
        the pieces of soul.

Soeurs d'étroit

Three hundred years of red retreat
before the stride of seeking feet
where cold relentless waters pour
the battered body of our shore
made room for all who came
to trap to cut to mine to stamp

O copper sisters of the earth
crystal sisters of the snow
cinnamon sisters of the sun
she was our motherland

An end of easy ways to please
contagious terror strange disease
youth beauty life all leaching out
retreat turned into rednecked rout
blind scabrous tenements
their victims' fault their testaments

O copper sisters of the earth
crystal sisters of the snow
cinnamon sisters of the sun
she is our sisterland

Remove the rags then salve the scars
return the gifts she lost not ours
but given to our blood to know
the wisdom of earth sun and snow
reminded by her plight
renew her flow her liquid life

O copper sisters of the earth
crystal sisters of the snow
cinnamon sisters of the sun
lift up our daughterland

Ancestors

we're all immigrants one time another
we were here however it happened
we did survive in you anyway
left you all

pushing and shoving at one another
molecules rearranging yourselves
into the new going to places
no one imagined

same as we did and you being part
of coincidence happens to be the
payment we need
if we get paid

for what it cost us to leave you here
our butterfly effect in time
what you are son
is our legacy

Neglect

Mama pretty sick
see him where they
beautiful they
not like us they
pretty rich they
live out there
they not want us

Mama pretty sick
don't got no way to
pay that way be
wrong way out for
us be in the way
he live out there
they beautiful

Mama better say she
go buy zantium

Call it research

you never know where it's going to be
a cookbook an art book or in sci-fi
like building blocks or puzzle pieces
in here somewhere collect enough
and after a time you have put together a
way of life from notions that people
leave lying about look through windows
look for what's striking strange and cool
you'll know when you see it steal this idea

Internet Nazis

Listen, girlfriend, leave it alone. They been
with us forever, think of themselves as
warriors, and you know soldiers, always fighting the
last damn war.

Yeah, I know, hanging from lampposts, but
give me a break. Look around you, girl. You
see any lampposts? Didn't happen by
accident.

Lurking's one thing. Go head, lurk. Plenty of time.
It's not like those bozos – no offense
to professional clowns – could get it up,
a fighting force, you know what I mean.

After all, they got no idea of their history.
What those fools do not know about aryan, nordic,
caucasian, and white – among other things –
well, it's good for a laugh.

And don't point out, how many of them are just like
me, some slavic genes – if they could think
about it, they wouldn't – along with the afro that
everyone's got.

You want to turn them, I guess it's okay, a
pilot test. I trust you, girl, you're too
smart to get caught. Don't believe in
cyberspace.

Worst case, you get us in trouble, we
break out the virus. You know which one
I'm talking about.

Genesis

We lost the garden to furied wind.
We were curious, hungry, fated to
learn. From savanna grass, we looked
back at fallen trees of evil, good,

of death, of life. We lived and
knew we would die, we were good
and we did great evil. We did not
disobey the rules by which we

came to be. After wind, the
wilderness. Without wild, without
water, soil, seeds and clay, no brick
to build a garden wall, no garden, and no

gardener. Leave the wild alone. That
is the test. Twisted winds of good and
evil, life and death, begin to gust
again. Let us not be tricked

again: there never was a wall.
Let us go back to the garden. Let us
go back to the garden and build ourselves a
gated wall and go out by another gate.

Poème noire

Beneath where towered poisons rise
to meld with reddened, lidded skies,
and cylinders of steelbound glass
are set aglow by neon gas,

deep in precincts of the night
the flash and howl of succor's might
recede and leave these rain-slicked streets
to us, who walk the oldest beats.

Call them john or call them mark,
names count for nothing in the dark,
escorted by Coyote's pack,
teeth bared to placate or attack.

No safety lies in hotel room,
no number can preclude the doom,
no stale and binding roles and rules
alert acculturated fools.

Blind as lemmings, blinder than,
because they are the sons of man,
they come before we summon them
to tapdance to their requiem.

a/k/a Satori

Death happens. Don't make it
worse, go out and do it
deliberately.

Look,
girlfriends, we know what
they did, we hear what you
say. I understand the
rage in your hearts. But
that's how it is. They got the
power was handed down, they
use it against us. Make 'em a
ghetto, a box to keep all their
hatreds and fears. You got a lid,
you need somebody to keep it on.

Why us? Cause we're
different from them. That's the
way the human brain works – ain't
what you're used to, it's best to be
scared. Trouble is, fear's an
adrenaline high, tends to stay
in the blood too long. And hate
bites back. You want to hate us?
Give you something to hate us about.

What it is, it's the wrong damn road. All
it leads to, another dead end, all shrunk
up on a reservation. After a while,
they don't even need the city
line. The ghetto we're
trapped in is all in our
heads.

Don't get me wrong, got nothing
against 'em, ghettoes and
reservations, that is. They
make real handy
places to hide.

All I'm saying, we gotta think
big. Jump the fences, whatever they are.
They want us to stay where we belong? Fine
with me. Where we belong is
Universe.

Answer me this. We
gonna be stuck here or
we gonna Jump?

Never too late (Madrugada)

When patterned life
becomes routine, makes
sheer celebrity required
for stature in the masses' eyes, and
crowded ladders standardize
the heights to which you
have aspired, when Everest
is a littered scene,

then go you into fortune's
way by hidden routes that
parallel the ditches deepened
by the herd, and pay you then
the price incurred, and
be you then the infidel who
braves the dawn of darker day.

In time beyond, the promise land
becomes the world that we command.

End of beginning

Wispy fingers across her face –
full moon child
laughing at us.

Otherwise

A century of centuries they never knew the
otherwise. Nor we. We called them wives of men,
we treasured, we distrusted them, we disallowed another
wise. Still, the otherwise is here. The turn was
made six lives ago and this time memory serves.
The woman known as Ma said Yes to what she had, to
what she was, the way that she was made. MaYa – the
daughter of wyfman and man's technology.

And m'an is not. So Maya says. If we could force – as we
have seen from years ago and places far from Here – if
we could make ourselves less rare, they'd have to
treasure us much less, they'd have to trust us
more. We'd have our fathers' freedoms back, the
cut, the run of earth, and ancient wilding ways.
But curves are made for taking, corners must be turned,
and this side of the spiral's theirs – after all, fair's fair.

Department of Deconstruction

Members of the Council, Ma'am:
herewith our annual report.

You will recall that in your second
winter session of last year
you ordinanced that any building
left unused for five full revolutions
of the sun no longer served the
Commonwealth. Houses, offices,
and shops, abandoned, dissipate
our energies. If, you said, the
building has no use to those who
had its price, it has no use to
anyone. We were instructed
to observe the onset of disease,
to seize depreciating property from
flagging private hands, to tear it
down, return it to the public good,
its highest and best use.

It gives us satisfaction to report
that, in the year-long span, some
ninety-five commercial spaces,
forty factories, and ten thousand
thirty-nine single family homes
have been removed. Materials have
been recovered and reused and
infrastructures capped and sealed.
These were, of course, constructions
of the modern kind, designed with
human productivity in mind, designed
to be in need of things, for maximum
consumption.

Of these spaces in our midst,
three have been requested for
location of new habitats;

you have approved; members of
those hands and bands and guilds
are meeting with the architects
and engineers. Our department
takes great pride in what has been
achieved. We have helped to
clear our land and make it right
for new designs that rightly make
our people.

The other lots, we're pleased to
say, have been enclosed to keep
investment out. An inventory
of these plots, these glades and
leas, shows thirteen different
kinds of bird; raccoons and
possum thrive among the weeds;
and, Council members, none too
soon, eleven types of trees.

Council members, we believe
complexity has been well served.
These lands no longer held our stores of
human energy. They have been returned,
restored, to Universe's trust, to her
instinctive density, wherein we find our
common wealth, our highest and best use.

Is he the one?

Is he the one? I know we've found him on the
hill and held him there, his body
strong and sweet and satisfied.

Is he the one? I know we've learned the
rhythms of the ways he lives with us,
his work is true and generous.

Is he the one? I know we've seen him when
a day's gone wrong, his anger hard and
hurtful, undissolved.

Is he the one? I know if I had him alone
a lifetime's length, his ways would
grow to overtake my days.

Is he the one? I know we four may leave
this hand when our children all are
made. Will he have stayed?

If he's the one, I know the wild receding
trace of time will add to these
more iridescent memories.

He is the one. I would have him
in this hand. We'll make his bands.

Everybody knows

Everybody knows that Kennet and Nyeli, salt and pepper, fierce
and fey, join hands; their mothers have been allies, they are friends,
their daughters in a hand the nearest thing to sisters that we have.

And everybody knows two more ordinary maya have been found to
balance and to anchor this inevitable pair, and now they know that
Kennet and Nyeli handfast our dear sweet Kath and ordinary me.

Everybody knows that for us four Kennet chooses Rodrhi. He's said yes,
how could he not, his line was always meant for hers, although they
both are sen, with whom they band they might not notice, even care.

And everybody knows that this is good: in May we will band Rodrhi, then
the little maya come, and when the daughters all are here, it's his turn for
a son. And everybody knows which one he'll ask, but sometimes recently

I've seen him watch Nyeli, and seen her not watch him, and Kennet never
notices. Sometimes I wonder when it's done, when we disband, will it
have been the kind of happy, ordinary hand that everybody knows?

Reclaimers' Hall

We come here to conceive, deliver, graduate, to
hand and band, dissolve, and die. She is the
center of our city state within a state. Outside,

the center city was often on an edge and only called
the center if wealthy and if white. When aged,
impoverished and dark, explosion, conflagration,

and center then was inner city, zero value, zero
ground. Desolated twisted forms survived on
toxic waste inside the rising, whitening ring.

Bureaucratic nightingales sang sympathetic songs
which soured into great grand mothers' howls of
rage and reclamation. Great thoughts while

waiting. Here my daughter comes to take from
four and six and eight decades the burden of
the life we've borne from birth. Delivered

by her hand, she takes my hand, and turns
to face my mother who took mine and looks at
Grand, the elders who alone of us know

who the father is. Deep within the halls,
the inner guardians of the lines protect,
preserve the gifts of m'an. They taught her

during testing years ago what she'll do now. I
remember I was terrified, alone in Matrix Hall.
The weight of all the long and winding routes

since even Africa lay on me. Momentum of
millennia of lines pushed me down a path whose
end I could not see. This is the only ceremony

we go through alone. When she's back and held in
loving hands, loneliness won't start to fade
for five slow months, until a quick and inner life

elicits dazzled laughs. At last we'll all return
with her, a bloody, joyous summer day. In Her
lovely centered hall, looking out on treasured

ground, we'll see my daughter and grand daughter
hold each other tightly and face their lives
with newborn cries of rage and reclamation.

No idea

What I found out
you got no idea
how much of what it
is you are what you think
about yourself what you
believing you should do
how much of that gets
pushed on you by
other people who got no
idea what it is they
doing to you maybe
they do maybe I do
some pushing myself
but I'm telling you
m'an you got no idea
how much till it's
gone

sometime I miss it
sometime I don't

I tell you what's better
than push is
pull

Draw down the lines

not mosaic color blocks but separate threads
unwinding as we find them single
straight or multi
plyed

tromp as writ no thread to spare and
each essential to the whole no
excessive careless knots to
worry at or
cut away

no tribe no kin true
mother lines single
hand to single hand
through warp and
weft of generations

my grand mother yours to me to
you and now within you strands
uncoil from unknown fathers
twisting strength from
great grand
mothers'
lines

a fragile family exposed
to time and wear may fade
and fray and break but still
the larger fabric holds and those who
are not sisters are not aunts
will gather and will mend

Abstract considerations

Tell me that we are not mad
when all the world minutely sprawls and
spreads an inch beyond the way it was
why must we make the giant leap
stride eastward to the sun

Complexity and density and
faith in rationality we cannot live
like this tell me that we are not
mad to try to hold our own
against disintegration

We are not mad where there is
faith in reason accidents are understood
skated over built upon foundations
fall new spider webs are spun to
trap and bridge eternity

We have temptation and romance
desire and birth and quest and death we
are not mad we do not live without
the chance to hold our own
her diaper needs changing

At one time this was a public park

a good enough place for a
m'an to stand let the emptiness
fall upon you fill itself
with the past that was

look across the river of time
see the other side of the future
make your choice about
stay or go

When smoke surrounds the birch

Steeped blue, the evening sky
spreads ink about our village lawn,
occludes the scattered families,
shrinks our world to only five.
The children close and chatter on,
are gathered up and taken in.
Night begins.

Three left, and you. As silence falls,
you shed the ways we see you live.
Daddy goes, then engineer,
Eiran's son, sweet volunteer,
until beneath an unseen tree
waits only m'an.

Nyeli's night. We other two
absorb the possibilities,
and in our sight her power grows.
She draws you in to dark through light.
When smoke surrounds the birch,
great flames ignite.

Non placet

Two days before the solstice we've come down
to where the emerald sea entreats a paper shore, where
gentle whitewashed green assaults the sandy rise, then pleads
with twisted trees for welcome and for rest in shallow inland pools.

We two, alone. You know what I will ask, I know you will say no. We
never meant our lives to be like this. I chose, was chosen by our
mothers' aristocracy for her. You chose her too, envisioning
a dynasty of daughters, but not, but not my son.

My son, my one, my only one, but who is he, how will he
look? Like her, like me, a fair square face and gray green
eyes, her sunlit hair, pure crystalline, from out of northwind's
lines. It's what we all of us have always seen. I know it will be so.

Ah, but he could share magnificence, the height of star flung skies, the
suntrapped strength of midnight pines, an austral skin and earthen
eyes, or maybe blue, the temper of our braided lines, if I could
give him what I've found, if I could give him you. You won't

agree. You say that what I want from you, your warmth, your
strength, your surety, would not survive your sacrifice of old
ancestral clarity. Look, the green has turned to gray. The steady
surging wind becomes a sea-born gale; frustrated breakers crash in rage

on unrelenting shore. Ruins built too close appear, remnants of an unwise
wish to have unending sun. Along the gulf they're everywhere outside
the trees, these battered traces of a m'an's desire, erected
even while we know they'll fall to storms at sea.

To Talis at eleven

Welcome, loom, embrace or crush,
these walls confront my child,
these polished floors, these
desks, the stage, the tool shop,
the cots, old ghostly voices,
corners friends create.

This is a gate, this building and the years:
beyond again the gardened land and then the wild
and on beyond – the stars to those who reach.

Municipal Building Code

This simplest of all litanies
admits of no prolonged debate:
there are no externalities.

All persons, matter, energies,
despite design, co-operate.
This simplest of all litanies

applies in all economies.
There's nothing we can isolate.
There are no externalities.

Approved designs have qualities
that elegantly illustrate
this simplest of all litanies.

Rejected schemes do injuries,
intrude, despoil, contaminate.
There are no externalities.

Show measure, rhythm, reason, please.
Be sure your plans incorporate
this simplest of all litanies.
There are no externalities.

Markings

girlchild Nzenga's
slender legs
among the reeds
a heron

old bricks   great trees
as yet unknown to
druids

the one I cannot
mother is my own –

Have you never thought that
some dark day
we'll find he is not Here?

tumbleweeds of lightning roll
over sleeping habitats
thunderstrikes explode give chase
dragging the drumbeats of blanketing rain

Helios the generous – no
wonder Gaia loves you

where chemistry does
not exist
let silence
seek
compassion

robins
suddenly
hop in the sun
springtime kernels
beginning to
pop

It's always all about the
children.
We make the place they
live in order to
make them.

It is as it is
and in no other way

Converso

You know they told us, ain't gonna work, we
don't got diversity. Askin' you, m'an, can you
tell it's there? Pull back, learn to listen,
a lot like huntin', my granddaddy said.

Ask *you*, m'an, who is this *we?*

The making of our days

These are the foundations of all that we are,
      the red and the green and the black.
These are the histories brought to our task,
      the copper, the crystal, the gold.
These the traditions that wind through our ways,
      our hands and our habs and our lines.
These the returns that we owe to our own,
      the kath and the kel and the sen.

These are the gifts we devote to our goal,
      the kath and the kel and the sen.
These are the threads on the loom of our days,
      our hands and our habs and our lines.
These are the braidings that strengthen our grasp,
      the copper, the crystal, the gold.
And these, these the steps on our reach to the stars,
      the red and the green and the black.

Father of the m'an

If I stopped leaning on this rail and slowly straightened
in the summer sun and raised the line and bob above
the lake and flipped them toward the rocky pools beside,

I'd catch the seventh year of that small boy. He'd take
the lure and pull away from endless exploration, a laughing
golden wriggling fish, his father's trophy catch.

If he and I stepped into that old boat and pushed away, we
wouldn't find the farther side of this great lake. We'd drift
atop tremendous rolling history from snow heaped melt pulled

south through narrow boundary. We'd turn and tumble over
cliffs and pass a thousand islands and lose our sight of
land where wide gray gulf salutes a northern sea.

If instead we walked and walked west from the shore, we'd find
miles of quiet farms. Concealed by gold of August wheat, storm
blackened prairie summer sky, green of tree and red of barn,

deep devotion to the tribal task, patient preservation of a
corridor that runs to home, cultivation of the glide where
now geese land, runway of the deer, tomorrow's launch.

If water way, our home would cast no anchor and no hook of
long drawn dreams. Carried past our starting point, we'd
float on individuality, going where we think we will alone.

If by the landward route, we'll find ourselves endstopped
within the family net in which we are both line and knot,
our places patterned by the mothers that I chose.

If otherwise than all the years that bring me to these points
of endless redecision, what ancient forms, what unknown
obligations, what other structures of approved desire

would form his days? What ghosts of glory call to him
from just beyond the wall, and who's to say they're
better than this sunlit life of loyal opposition?

Eliane

Trapped by desires unseeing
caught as I wished to be caught
one with my one and her two and our three
and distant dangerous angry Eliane

Years lost to dailiness fleeing
all Maya's lessons untaught
ever untouched by her harsh mystery
and distant dangerous angry Eliane

Tonight understanding awakened
will not tolerate absence of love
or hate in the darkness descended
on distant dangerous angry Eliane

Make hate to me let me be taken
for the fool that I made a fool of
make hate for the years that have ended
my distant dangerous angry Eliane

Blackberry moon

august night –
shadows, crickets, barking
dog two blocks away –
wrap your arms around me

The ceremony to disband: Nyeli does not speak

It's always all about the children,
these hands, these bands, these
marriages of ours. It's not
supposed to be for life

or love, but brief intent, some
nineteen years to reproduce
our lines and make our
children strong and

brave and free to carry on,
continue and complete the
dream that Matrix has of
us, our dance of coming

home. We've done it well.
This early morning they
are here with us, four
maya, one young m'an,

to celebrate what they
and we've become, to mark
the end of childhood, the
loosening of promises

and bonds, when we move on
to wider times and space,
a letting go of hands.
Kennet climbs imagined

heights – she may forget to
sleep. Her Talis is our
first, she's found her
hand, they'll band next

year, and when it's done,
she'll do that thing that
Kennet's always dreamed.
My Nzenga, not a kel like

me turned outward to the
world, she looks within
for better ways to
supersede the old,

she's just as fierce as
all our line about the
truth she finds. And
Kath will always be

right Here: where Kath
is, they'll call home.
Her Alyn, rebel of
their line, is

bound to be a kel. Eliane,
perceptive one, has gone
beyond our hand; she'll
join the guild her

friends have formed; my
brother Adam joins it too,
he's told me, when he's
free, and that's for Eliane,

he says. It deeply pleases me.
Eli's Beth, our youngest girl,
so like her mother now, but
kath all through: I hope

she'll go where Talis leads for
memory of home. And Niall,
clearly Rodrhi's son, a
seeker – a dreamer like

his mother too. The flight that
Talis makes, I think, will be
on Niall's wings. I'll be
where I've been so long,

out at the edge, trader, guard,
and diplomat, one of those
who make the space for
all the lives they

lead. Now we're nearly at the
end, we've undone Rodrhi's
bands. This is truly
letting go,

letting go of center, a center
that has held us through the
years with grace and strength
and dignity. Aie, Rodrhi,

I've never spoken of that day,
I've done some necessary
things, I've had to, I
am kel. Denying you

has always been –
it's true, the
recent lines of
Africa run through me –

the fire between us,
and a son, would have
destroyed our hand.
And you knew that. As

much as I, you are
guardian of the lines,
your restlessness
controlled, constrained,

in service to our goal.
You could, you should
be kel. Yet grandmothers
never trust our borders to

a m'an. The guardians
mistrust the m'an they
made. I do not. Historic
wrong is not well righted by

reversal. Tonight you'll walk
away from us and go in search
of some new compromise with
what you are. The narrow

boundaries you find will be
the measure of a disappointed
life. You are kel and not
allowed to be. Aie, Rodrhi –

Aground

Midnight. Atop the cutter's mast the huge klieg
stares implacably, unmoved by long drowned
frozen scream as what I thought I was
is wrecked and lost on your uncharted shore.

Outside the cone of cold blue light, refuge
rejected, wrapped in icy northborn howl,
you stand apart. Your hand unfolds
reluctantly, directs the mind behind the glare

to search, to look for life. The
light that falls becomes a sun, a vast
contaminated radiance of love.

Winter sun

They haven't got the numbers right, Out There
where she died. Slouching toward
pornography,

> drums and wind and
> howling rage ice the heart
> breaking under
> winter sun

they undermine our destiny. That is where
I've got to go, unpromising though
the prospect is, carrying seeds

> storm and sleet
> and dying light

of what she was, invisible weeds to break them down.
Despite what they say, you will go with me. I will
know what, and you will know how.

> the gale will
> end tonight the
> sky will clear and the
> sun come up

She named me for an African queen, one who knew how
to make good use of warriors. I have often wondered
about that m'an. Do you know the story?

> yes but
> not because
> she told me

> So. The wind dies down.
> We will leave Here, when the
> sun comes up.

A song at the edge of nonlinear space

Straight lines and climbing trends
describe observed stability
define the past statistically
so grow so rise so centralize
deliberate modernity

or shrink or scatter deconstruct
and fluctuate chaotically
through cyclic creativity
within progressive entropy
dance and drift and realize
forevers flow dynamically

outside a central tendency
extreme eccentric ecstasy
catastrophe
and our responsibility
lets patterns of integrity
equilibrate equilibrate
about a
moving
point

.

Open to interpretation

be elsewhere
travel light
one and the same time

currents eddies electrical storms
struck as if by lightning as if

the map is not the territory
except when it is when it's inside your head

topography topology disaster or catastrophe
difference makes a convenient clock

Gaia, Matrix, Universe
grab onto the monkey bars
Universal jungle gym

after heat EZ cool
detach yourself
under pressure EZ to jump

closer to gravity close to warmth
float to the surface
everywhere time the infinite pulse

the microcosm shall always be with you
try to think it's the good
that survives

a mistake to believe there is absence of time
necessity's a mother

Ice, fire, water falls . . .

Will you come with us tomorrow to watch
the end of our time in this innocent space
come with us we made them we send them away
into the infinite why

Will you come with us we need you again
our dreams die above us we no longer wait
we need you our future is falling on us
out of a desolate sky

Piloting, the craft

Completely aside from any consideration of history – or
herstory, due deference to those who taught and
spoke and wrote when they should have cut and run, who
missed the chance to mother us –

and aside from issues of political effect – although,
She knows, times will become exceedingly
interesting once it's realized just
whose colony is looking back at them –

and also aside from any evolutionary significance
this mission holds, not to mention my own
responsibility for those aboard in my command,

to do this job, to perch within this fragile metal
shell, withdrawn from huge reality, watching through
these widened windowed eyes the face behind the void,
attending to the subtle signs of attitude and stress,

to feel within the alternating pauses of attained
plateaus and course corrections powered by
deep vibratory jets, to get it right by careful
timing, practiced touch – it's nothing new,

it's mostly like the mastery of m'an on earth,
with no small similarity to giving easy birth.

Echoes of a creed

Beloved sister of the starred sky,
Universe is waiting for your cry,
awaiting Gaia's child.

> we can build a
> world
> we can

> *red*
> that is good for the
> people and
> *green*
> that is good
> for the planet and
> *black* that is good
> for tomorrow

let's declare girls' rules, and girlfriend village

Matrix aid Matrix made
In me She makes Herself

> We gonna be stuck here
> or we gonna Jump?

Anything that happens is okay.
It is as it is, and in no other way.

Acknowledgements

These speakers have many ancestors, among them

C. J. Cherryh
for the concept of kath, kel, and sen
in her trilogy 'The Faded Sun'

Dennis Schmidt
for the vision of jump
in the 'Wayfarer' books

Cynthia Shelby-Lane, MD
for putting a name to girlfriend village

and

the ladies from the Caribbean
for the friendship and lending structure known as a hand
(an opposing thumb is my own addition)

*'Was it some anthropologist,
maybe Margaret Mead, who said
that any society's main challenge is
figuring out what to do
with its males?'*

you'll know when you see it

Thank you for reading *Promise Land: Voices From a Future Detroit*. If you liked the lyrics, or if you didn't, please visit your favorite book-finding site (mine is GoodReads) and write a brief review. Your feedback is important to me and will help other readers decide whether to read the book too.

If you'd like to get notifications of new releases and special offers on my books, please join my email list at LeeDennis.com.

Lee Dennis
lives and works in Detroit under another name

www.ingramcontent.com/pod-product-compliance
Lightning Source LLC
Chambersburg PA
CBHW060617030426
42337CB00018B/3085